Courage

Courage: Timeless Thoughts of Bravery to Shield You in a Changing World
Edited by Clinton Galloway

Published by Phoenix Publishing Corp.

Cover and interior design by
Lee Lewis, Words+Design, 888-883-8347

Manufactured in the United States of America

ISBN 0-9708860-3-9

Additional copies may be ordered by sending $12.95, check or money order, to:

Phoenix Publishing Corp.
P.O. Box 10325
Marina Del Rey, CA 90295

Visit our website at www.phxpub.com

Courage

Timeless Thoughts of Bravery to Shield You in a Changing World

Edited by
Clinton Galloway

Phoenix Publishing Corp.
Marina Del Rey, California

for your inscription, dedication, and comments

When you get into a tight place, and everything goes against you, till it seems as if you couldn't hold on a minute longer, never give up then, for that's just the place and time that the tide'll turn.

— *Harriet Beecher Stowe*

The hero is no braver than the ordinary man, but he is brave five minutes longer.

— *Ralph Waldo Emerson*

Have courage for the great sorrows of life and patience for the small ones; when you have laboriously accomplished your daily task go to sleep in peace. God is awake.

— *Victor Marie Hugo*

The bad man's courage still prepares the way for its own outwitting.

— *Samuel T. Coleridge*

The block of granite which is an obstacle in the pathway of the weak, becomes a stepping stone in the pathway of the strong.

— *Thomas Carlyle*

Remember that if the opportunities for great needs should never come, the opportunity for good deeds is renewed day by day. The thing for us to long for is the goodness, not the glory.

— Frederick William Faber

"Though I cannot teach courage," said Nekayah, "I must not learn cowardice."

— *Samuel Johnson*

We must build dikes of courage to hold back the flood of fear.

— *Martin Luther King, Jr.*

Courage and perseverance have a magic talisman, before which difficulties disappear and obstacles vanish into air.

— *John Quincy Adams*

It is curious that physical courage should be so common in the world and moral courage so rare.

— *Mark Twain*

Courage is the best gift of all; courage stands before everything. It is what preserves our liberty, safety, life, and our homes and parents, our country and children. Courage comprises all things; a man with courage has every blessing.

— *Plautus*

A man of courage never wants weapons.

— *Thomas Fuller*

The greatest test of courage on the earth is to bear defeat without losing heart.

— *Robert G. Ingersoll*

Who, then, is the invincible man? He whom nothing outside the sphere of his moral purpose can dismay.

— *Epictetus*

Courage is a special kind of knowledge; the knowledge of how to fear what ought to be feared and how not to fear what ought to be feared.

— *David Ben-Gurion*

No coward soul is mine,
No trembler in the world's
storm-troubled sphere;
I see Heaven's glories shine,
And Faith shines equal, arming
me from fear.

— *Emily Bronte*

O, fear not in a world like this
  And thou shalt know erelong,
Know how sublime a thing it is
  To suffer and be strong.

— Henry Wadsworth Longfellow

No, when the fight begins within himself,
A man's worth something. God stoops
o'er his head.

— Robert Browning

That's courage - to take hard knocks like a man when occasion calls.

— Plautus

Thus I resolved on—to run, when I can, to go, when I cannot run; and to creep, when I cannot go.

— John Bunyan

We try to grasp too much of life at a time. We think of it as a whole, instead of taking the days one by one. Life is a mosaic, and each tiny piece must be cut and set with skill.

— *Anonymous*

He hath borne himself beyond the promise of his age, doing, in the figure of a lamb, the feats of a lion.

— William Shakespeare

Courage is fear that has said its prayers.

— Dorothy Bernard

Courage is poorly housed that dwells in numbers; the lion never counts the herd that are about him, nor weighs how many flocks he has to scatter.

— Aaron Hill

Courage is imperial. It underlies true achievement. Unless we have moral nerve to live out our convictions, they are of small account.

— Anonymous

There is courage in the treatment of every art by a master in architecture, in sculpture, in painting or in poetry, each cheering the mind of the spectator or receiver as by true strokes of genius, which yet nowise implies the presence of physical valor in the artist. This is the courage of genius in every kind.

— *Ralph Waldo Emerson*

True courage is to do without witnesses everything that one is capable of doing before all the world.

— *Duc de la Rochefoucauld*

Courage is the scorner of things which inspire fear.

— *Seneca*

The difference between talents and character is adroitness to keep the old and trodden round, and power and courage to make a new road to new and better goals.

— *Ralph Waldo Emerson*

If Winter comes, can Spring be far behind?

— *Percy Bysshe Shelley*

To be always intending to lead a new life, but never to find time to set about it; this is as if a man should put off eating and drinking and sleeping from one day and night to another, till he is starved and destroyed.

— *John Tillotson*

To fight aloud is very brave,
But gallanter, I know,
Who charge within the bosom
The Calvary of woe.

— Emily Dickinson

Woman and men of retiring timidity are cowardly only in dangers which affect themselves, but first to rescue when others are in danger.

— Jean Paul Richter

He who loses wealth loses much, he who loses a friend loses more, but he that loses courage loses all.

— Dana Gatlin

Nothing but courage can guide life.

— Luc de Clapiers Vauvenargues

Courage, the highest gift, that
scorns to bend
To mean devices for a sordid end,
Courage—an independent spark
from Heaven's bright throne,
By which the soul stands raised,
triumphant,
High, alone...

— *George Farquhar*

Courage, the footstool of the Virtues, upon which they stand.

— Robert Louis Stevenson

Live as though life were earnest, and life will be so.

— Owen Meredith

Many owe the grandeur of their lives to their tremendous difficulties.

— Charles Haddon Spurgeon

God will come in at the deepest part of the stream to lend you a hand.

— Samuel Rutherford

It is good to know; it is better to do; it is best to be. To be pure and strong, to be honest and earnest, to be kindly and thoughtful, and in all to be true, to be manly and womanly. He can do more for others who has done most with himself.

— *Samuel Dickey Gordon*

'Tis more brave
To live, than to die.

— Owen Meredith

Where in the heart there is combined love and courage, even the weak become mighty.

— Harold Whaley

Fortitude I take to be the quiet possession of a man's self, and an undisturbed doing his duty whatever evils beset, or dangers lie in the way.

— John Locke

Courage is fire, and bullying is smoke.

— Benjamin Disraeli

There are degrees of courage and each step upward makes us acquainted with a higher virtue. Let us say then frankly that the education of the will is the object of our existence.

— Ralph Waldo Emerson

True courage is not the brutal force of vulgar heroes, but the firm resolve of virtue and reason.

— *William Whitehead*

Sing unto the Lord a new song; sing praises lustily unto him with a good courage.

— *Book of Common Prayer*

True courage scorns
To vent her prowess in a storm of words;
And, to the valiant, actions speak alone.

— *Tobias George Smollet*

A brave captain is as a root, out of which, as branches, the courage of his soldiers doth spring.

— *Sir Philip Sidney*

the joy of a manly
selfhood!
To be servile to none,
to defer to none, not
to any tyrant known and
unknown,
To walk with erect carriage, a step
springy and elastic,
To look with calm gaze or with a
flashing eye.

— *Walt Whitman*

The brave man is not he who feels no fear, for that were stupid and irrational; but he whose noble soul subdues its fear, and bravely dares the danger nature shrinks from.

— *Joanna Baillie*

Be strong and of good courage; be not afraid, neither be thou dismayed: for the Lord thy God is with thee whithersoever thou goest.

— *Joshua 1:9*

The greater the difficulty, the more glory in surmounting it. Skillful pilots gain their reputation from storms and tempests.

— *Epicurus*

Man who would be,
Must rule the empire of himself; in it
Must be supreme, establishing his throne,
Of vanquished will, quelling the anarchy
Of hopes and fears, being himself alone.

— Percy Bysshe Shelley

Physical bravery is an animal instinct; moral bravery is a much higher and truer courage.

— *Wendell Phillips*

There is nothing in the world so much admired as a man who knows how to bear unhappiness with courage.

— *Seneca*

Courage is to do without witnesses what one would be capable of doing with the world looking on.

— *Francois De La Rochefoucald*

In great attempts it is glorious even to fail.

— *Longinus*

The characteristic of a genuine heroism is its persistency. All men have wandering impulses, fits and starts of generosity. But when you have resolved to be great, abide by yourself, and do not weakly try to reconcile yourself with the world. The heroic cannot be the common, nor the common the heroic.

— *Ralph Waldo Emerson*

Some men give up their designs when they have almost reached the goal; while others, on the contrary, obtain a victory by exerting, at the last moment, more vigorous efforts than before.

— *Polybius*

Counsel that I once heard given to a young person, "Always do what you are afraid to do."

— *Ralph Waldo Emerson*

Experience shows that success is due less to ability than to zeal. The winner is he who gives himself to his work, body and soul.

— *Charles Buxton*

The gods always favor the strong.

— *Tacitus*

Oh, while I live to be the ruler of
life, not a slave,
To meet life as a powerful
conqueror,
No fumes, no ennui, no more
complaints, or criticisms,
To these proud laws of the air, the
water and the ground,
Proving my interior soul
impregnable,
And nothing exterior shall ever
take command of me.

— *Walt Whitman*

The brave find a home in every land.

— Ovid

Courage brother! Do not stumble!
Though thy path is dark as night;
There's a star to guide the humble;
Trust in God, and do the Right!

— Norman MacLeod

A man should stop his ears against paralyzing terror, and run the race that is set before him with a single mind.

— Robert Louis Stevenson

Fortune and love favor the brave.

— Ovid

Moral courage is a virtue of higher cast and nobler origin than physical. It springs from a consciousness of virtue, and renders a man, in the pursuit or defense of right, superior to the fear of reproach, opposition, or contempt.

— *Samuel Griswold Goodrich*

However mean your life is, meet it and live it; do not shun it and call it hard names.

— Henry David Thoreau

Man is not the creature of circumstances; circumstances are the creatures of men.

— Benjamin Disraeli

I wonder is it because men are cowards in heart that they admire bravery so much, and place military valor so far beyond every other quality for reward and worship.

— William Thackeray

Self-trust is the essence of heroism.

— Ralph Waldo Emerson

When a resolute young fellow steps up to the great bully, the world, and takes him boldly by the beard, he is often surprised to find it comes off in his hand, and that it was only tied to scare away the timid adventurers.

— *Ralph Waldo Emerson*

When moral courage feels that it is in the right, there is no personal daring of which it is incapable.

— *Leigh Hunt*

It is not because things are difficult that we do not dare, it is because we do not dare that they are difficult.

— *Seneca*

The man who is just and resolute will not be moved from his settled purpose, either by the misdirected rage of his fellow citizens, or by the threats of an imperious tyrant.

— *Horace*

Doubt whom you will, but never yourself.

— *Christine Nestell Boveé*

The bravery founded on hope of recompense fear of punishment, experience of success, on rage, or on ignorance of danger, is but common bravery, and does not deserve the name. True bravery proposes a just end; measures the dangers, and meets the result with calmness and unyielding decision.

— Francois de la Noue

Courage consists not in blindly overlooking danger, but in seeing it and conquering it.

— *Jean Paul Richter*

The heights by great men reached and
kept,
Were not attained by sudden flight,
But they, while their companions slept,
Were toiling upward in the height.

— *Henry Wadsworth Longfellow*

Courage makes a man more than himself; for he is then himself plus his valor.

— *William Rounseville Alger*

Character is singularly contagious.

— *Samuel A. Eliot*

The estimate and valor of a man consists in the heart and in the will; there his true honor lies. Valor is stability, not of arms and legs, but of courage and the soul; it does not lie in the valor of our horse, nor of our arms, but in ourselves. He that falls obstinate in his courage, if his legs fail him, fights upon his knees.

— *Michel De Montaigne*

Courage! Suffering, when it climbs highest, lasts not long.

— *Aeschylus*

Those who believe that the praises which arise from valor are superior to those which proceed from any other virtues have not considered.

— *John Dryden*

Be not merely good; be good for something.

— *Henry David Thoreau*

The Lord is my light and my salvation; whom shall I fear? The Lord is the strength of my life; of whom shall I be afraid?

— *Psalm 27*

A man must have the gift to discern at all turns where the true heart of the matter lies and to plant himself courageously on that, as a strong man that other true men may rally round him there. He will not continue leader of men otherwise.

— *William Carlyle*

Ye fearful saints fresh courage take,
The clouds ye so much dread
Are big with mercy, and shall break
In blessings on your head.

— *William Cowper*

I know of no more encouraging fact than the unquestionable ability of man to elevate his life by a conscious endeavor.

— *Henry David Thoreau*

This is another day! Are its eyes blurred
With maudlin grief for any wasted past?
A thousand thousand failures shall not
  daunt!
Let dust clasp dust, death, death; I am
  alive!

— *Don Marquis*

Go to your work and be strong,
halting not in your ways,
Balking the end half-won, for an
instant's dole of praise.
Stand to your work and be wise,
certain of sword and pen,
Being neither children, nor gods,
but men in a world of men.

—*Rudyard Kipling*

Art little? Do thy little well,
And for they comfort know
Great men can do their greatest work
No better than just so.

— *Johann Wolfgang von Goethe*

Be not afraid of life. Believe that life is worth living and your belief will help create the fact.

— *William James*

Women and men of retiring timidity are cowardly only in dangers which affect themselves, but are the first to rescue when others are endangered.

— *Jean Paul Richter*

The better part of valor is discretion.

— *William Shakespeare*

If thou desire to be truly valiant, fear to do any injury; he that fears to do evil is always afraid to suffer evil; he that never fears is desperate; he that fears always is a coward; he is the true valiant man that dares nothing but what he may, and fears nothing but what he ought.

— *Francis Quarles*

Tender handed stroke a nettle,
And it stings you for your pains;
Grasp it like a man of mettle,
And it soft as silk remains.

— Aaron Hill

The eternal stars shine out as soon as it is dark enough.

— Thomas Carlyle

Courage that grows from constitution, often forsakes a man when he has occasion for it; courage which arises from a sense of duty acts in a uniform manner.

— Joseph Addison

The busy have no time for tears.

— Lord Byron

Write on your doors the saying
wise and old,
"Be bold!" and everywhere—
"Be bold;
Be not too bold!" Yet better the
excess
Than the defect; better the more
than less;
Better like Hector in the field to
die,
Than like a perfumed Paris turn
and fly.

— *Henry Wadsworth Longfellow*

A man must not complain of his "element," or of his "time," or the like; it is thriftless work doing so. His time is bad; well then, he is there to make it better.

— *Thomas Carlyle*

God gives each man one life, like a lamp,
 Then gives
That lamp due measure of oil: lamp
 lighted—
Hold high, wave wide
Its comfort of others to share.

— *Robert Browning*

The greatest object in the universe, says a certain philosopher, is a good man struggling with adversity; yet there is still greater, which is the good man that comes to relieve it.

— *Oliver Goldsmith*

Courage ought to be guided by skill, and skill armed by courage. Hardiness should not darken wit, nor wit cool hardiness. Be valiant as men despising death, but confident as unwonted to be overcome.

— *Sir Philip Sidney*

Let us be of good cheer, however, remembering that the misfortunes hardest to bear are those which never come.

— Oliver Wendell Holmes

True courage is not built upon mental cleverness, or earthly power, but it stands upon the solid rock of truth and spiritual power.

— Lowell Fillmore

Not in the clamor of the crowded street
Not in the shouts and plaudits of the
  throng
But in ourselves are triumph and defeat.

— Henry Wadsworth Longfellow

Every noble work is at first impossible.

— Thomas Carlyle

Unbounded courage and
compassion joined,
Tempering each other in the
victor's mind,
Alternately proclaim him good
and great,
And make the hero and the man
complete.

— *Joseph Addison*

Be strong, and quit yourselves like men.

— I Samuel, iv, 9

Nothing is too high for a man to reach, but he must climb with care and confidence.

— Hans Christian Andersen

Brave your storm with firm endeavor, let
your vain repinings go
Hopeful hearts will find forever
roses underneath your snow!

— James Fenimore Cooper

Be steadfast as a tower that doth not bend its stately summit to the tempest's shock.

— Dante

It is an error to suppose that courage means courage in everything. Most people are brave only in the dangers to which they accustom themselves, either in imagination or practice.

— *Edward George Bulwer-Lytton*

When fate is adverse, a wise man can always strive for happiness and sail against the wind to attain it.

— *Jean Jacques Rosseau*

I prefer to strive in bravery with the bravest, rather than in the wealth with the richest, or in greed with the greediest.

— *Marcus Caro*

Being a man, ne'er ask the gods for a life set free from grief, but ask for courage that endureth long.

— *Menander*

Wait on the Lord: be of good courage and he shall strengthen thine heart.

— *Psalm 27*

So in regard to disagreeable and formidable things, prudence does not consist in evasion or flight, but in courage. He who wishes to walk in the most peaceful parts of life with any serenity must screw himself up to resolution. Let him front the object of his worst apprehension, and his stoutness will commonly make his fear groundless.

— *Ralph Waldo Emerson*

Courage is resistance to fear, mastery of fear—not absence of fear.

— Mark Twain

It is better to die on your feet than to live on your knees.

— Emiliano Zapata

Courage consists not in hazarding without fear, but being resolutely minded in a just cause.

— Plutarch

Courage leads starward, fear toward death.

— Seneca

A high character might be produced, I suppose, by continued prosperity, but it has very seldom been the case. Adversity, however, it may appear to be our foe, is our true friend; and, after a little acquaintance with it, we receive it as a precious thing—the prophecy of a coming joy. It should be no ambition of ours to traverse a path without a thorn or stone.

— *Charles H. Spurgeon*

Most of the important things in the world have been accomplished by people who have gone on trying when there seemed to be no hope at all.

— *Dale Carnegie*

We all stand in the front rank of the battle every moment of our lives; where there is a brave man in the thickest of the fight, there is the point of honor.

— *Henry David Thoreau*

Fear to do base and unworthy things is valor; if they be done to us, to suffer them is also valor.

— *Ben Jonson*

The best hearts are ever the bravest.

— *Laurence Sterne*

The wisest man could ask no more
of fate
Than to be simple, modest, manly,
true,
Safe from the many, honored by
the few;
Nothing to court in Church, or
World, or State,
But inwardly in secret to be great.

— *James Russell Lowell*

Happiness is freedom, and freedom is courage.

— *Pericles*

The coward dies a thousand deaths, the valiant only once.

— *William Shakespeare*

He who loses wealth loses much; he who loses a friend loses more; but he that loses his courage loses all.

— *Miguel De Cervantes*

One day, with life and heart,
Is more than time enough to find a
world.

— *James Russell Lowell*

friends, be men, and
let your hearts be
strong,
And let no warrior in
the heat of fight
Do what may bring him shame in
others' eyes;
For more of those who shrink
from shame are safe
Than fall in battle, while with
those who flee
Is neither glory nor reprieve from
death.

— *Homer*

Through all the air the eagle may roam
The whole earth is father-land to the brave.

— *Ovid*

The only failure a man ought to fear is failure in cleaving to the purpose he sees to be best.

— *George Eliot*

Keep your fears to yourself, but share your courage with others.

— *Robert Louis Stevenson*

The two powers which in my opinion constitute a wise man are those of bearing and forbearing.

— *Epictetus*

As courage and intelligence are the two qualifications best worth a good man's cultivation, so it is the first part of intelligence to recognize our precarious estate in life, and the first part of courage to be not at all abashed before the fact.

— *Robert Louis Stevenson*

The coward threatens when he is safe.

— Johann Wolfgang Von Goethe

Courage is rightly esteemed the first of human qualities because it is the quality which guarantees all others.

— Winston Churchill

Be noble! And the nobleness that lies
In other men, sleeping, but never dead,
Will rise in majesty to meet thine own.

— Johann von Schiller

Courage is knowing what not to fear.

— Socrates

ou gain strength, courage and confidence by every experience in which you really stop to look fear in the face. You are able to say to yourself, "I have lived through this horror. I can take the next thing that comes along." You must do the thing you think you cannot.

— *Eleanor Roosevelt*

He is not worthy of the honeycomb
That shuns the hive because the bees have
stings.

— *William Shakespeare*

All brave men love; for he only is brave who has affections to fight for, whether in the daily battle of life, or in physical contests.

— *Nathaniel Hawthorne*

There are two freedoms: the false where one is free to do what he likes and the true where he is free to do what he ought.

— *Charles Kingsley*

Our aspirations are our possibilities.

— *Robert Browning*

That only which we have within, can we see without. If we meet no gods, it is because we harbor none. If there is grandeur in you, you will find grandeur in porters and sweeps. He only is rightly immortal, to whom all things are immortal. I have read somewhere, that none is accomplished, so long as any are incomplete; that the happiness of one cannot consist with the misery of any other.

— *Ralph Waldo Emerson*

From the lowliest depth there is a path to the loftiest height.

— *William Carlyle*

I beg you take courage; the brave soul can mend even disaster.

— *Catherine of Russia*

There's a brave fellow! There's a man of
  pluck!
A man who's not afraid to say his say,
Though a whole town's against him.

— *Henry Wadsworth Longfellow*

I am devilishly afraid, that's certain; but I'll sing, that I may seem valiant.

— *John Dryden*

No man is born into
the world,
whose work
Is not born with
him. There is always work
And tools to work withal, for
those who will:
And blessed are the thorny hands
of toil.

— *James Russell Lowell*

Hope awakens courage.
He who can implant courage in the
human soul
Is the best physician.

— Karl Ludwig Von Knebel

The great pleasure in life is doing what people say you cannot do.

— Walter Bagehot

As soon as you trust yourself, you will know how to live.

— Johann Wolfgang von Goethe

The burden which is well borne becomes light.

— Ovid

I have no fear! What is in store for me
Shall find me self-reliant, undismayed.
God grant my only cowardice may be
Afraid—to be afraid!

— *Everard Jack Appleton*

We always have time enough, if we use it aright.

— Johann Wolfgang von Goethe

Life is mostly froth and bubble,
Two things stand like stone—
Kindness in another's trouble,
Courage in ones own.

— Adam L. Gordon

A timid person is frightened before a danger, a coward during the time, and a courageous person afterward.

— Jean Paul Richter

For courage mounteth with occasion.

— William Shakespeare

True courage is cool and calm. The bravest of men have the least of a brutal, bullying insolence, and in the very time of danger are found the most serene and free.

— *Anthony Shaftsbury*

The courage we desire and prize is not the courage to die decently but to live manfully.

— *Thomas Carlyle*

When God shuts a door, he opens a window.

— *John Ruskin*

Unless above himself he can
Erect himself, how poor a thing is man!

— *Samuel Daniel*

To see what is right and not to do it, is want of courage.

— *Confucius*

Did you ever hear of a man who had striven all his life faithfully and singly toward an object, and in no measure obtained it? If a man constantly aspires, is he not elevated? Did a man try heroism, magnanimity, truth, sincerity, and find that there was no advantage to them—that it was a vain endeavor?

— *Henry David Thoreau*

The direct foe of courage is the fear itself, not the object of it, and the man who can overcome his own terror is a hero and more.

— *George Macdonald*

The sweetest music is not in the oratorio, but in the human voice when it speaks from its instant life tones of tenderness, truth or courage.

— *Ralph Waldo Emerson*

Courage is knowing what not to fear.

— *Plato*

A true knight is fuller of bravery in the midst, than in the beginning of danger.

— *Sir Philip Sidney*

e's truly valiant that
can suffer wisely
The worst that man
can breathe and
make his wrongs
His outsides, to wear them like
his raiment,
carelessly;
And ne'er prefer his injuries to
his heart
To bring it into danger.

— *William Shakespeare*

A great deal of talent is lost in this world for the want of a little courage.

— John Smith

Not failure, but low aim is a crime.

— James Russell Lowell

One man with courage makes a majority.

— Thomas Jefferson

Nothing can work me damage, except myself. The harm that I sustain I carry about me, and never am a real sufferer but by my own fault.

— St. Bernard

The brave man seeks not popular
applause,
Nor, overpower'd with arms,
deserts his cause;
Unsham'd, though foil'd, he does
the best he can,
Force is of brutes, but honor is of
man.

— *John Dryden*

To have what we want is riches; but to be able to do without is power.

— George Macdonald

No man can answer for his courage who has never been in danger.

— Duc de la Rochefoucauld

One self-approving hour whole years outweigh.

— Alexander Pope

The men who succeed best in public life are those who take the risk of standing by their own convictions.

— James A. Garfield

hysical courage which despises all danger, will make a man brave in one way; and moral courage, which despises all opinion, will make a man brave in another. The former would seem most necessary for the camp; the latter for the council; but to constitute a great man both are necessary.

— *Caleb C. Colton*

No man can produce great things who is not thoroughly sincere in dealing with himself.

— *James Russell Lowell*

Confidence or courage is conscious ability —the sense of power.

— *William Hazlitt*

In the most private life, difficult duty is never far off. Therefore we must think with courage.

— *Ralph Waldo Emerson*

Recall your courage, and lay aside sad fear.

— *Virgil*

The low man seeks a little to do,
Sees it and does it;
This high man, with a great thing to pursue,
Does ere he knows it.
That low man goes on adding one to one,
His hundred's soon hit;
This high man, aiming at a million,
Misses a unit,
That has the world here—should he need the next,
Let the world mind him!
This throws himself on God, and unperplexed,
Seeking shall find Him.

— *Robert Browning*

Courage knows no yielding to calamity.

— *Publilius Syrus*

A man must stand erect, not be kept erect by others.

— *Marcus Aurelius*

Who does the best his circumstance
allows,
Does well, acts nobly—angels could no
more.

— *Edward Young*

Be of good cheer: it is I; be not afraid.

— *Matthew 14:27*

To suffer woes which
hope thinks infinite;
To forgive wrongs
darker than the death
or night;
To defy power, which seems
omnipotent;
To love, to bear to hope till Hope
creates
From its own wreck, the things to
comtemplate;
Neither change, to falter, or
repent;
This, like the glory Titan, is to be
Good, great and joyous, beautiful
and free;
This is alone, Life, Joy, Empire,
and Victory.

— *Percy Bysshe Shelley*

It is in great dangers that we see great courage.

— Jean Regnard

A man of courage is also full of faith.

— Cicero

I count life just a stuff
To try the soul's strength on.

— Robert Browning

Endurance is the crowning quality, and patience all the passion of great hearts.

— James Russell Lowell

One who never turned his back
    but marched breast forward
Never doubted clouds would
    break
Never dreamed, though right were
    worsted,
wrong would triumph,
Held we fall to rise, are baffled to
    fight better,
Sleep to wake.

— *Robert Browning*

Presence of mind and courage in distress,
Are more than armies to procure success.

— *John Dryden*

Our only greatness is that we aspire.

— *Jean Ingelow*

To a brave man, good and bad luck are like his right and left hand. He uses both.

— *St. Catherine of Siena*

Courage conquers all things: it even gives strength to the body.

— *Ovid*

The first lesson of life is to burn our own smoke; that is, not to inflict on outsiders our personal sorrows and petty morbidness, not to keep thinking of ourselves as exceptional cases.

— *James Russell Lowell*

Courage from hearts, and not from numbers grows.

— *John Dryden*

Courage consists in equality to the problem before us.

— *Ralph Waldo Emerson*

The braver the man so much the more fortunate will he be.

— *Latin Proverb*

A brave man is clear in his discourse, and keeps close to truth.

— *Aristotle*

The ultimate measure of a man is not where he stands in moments of comfort and convenience, but where he stands in times of challenge and controversy.

— *Martin Luther King, Jr.*

The strongest is never strong enough to be always the master, unless he transforms his strength into right, and obedience into duty.

— Jean Jacques Rousseau

Courage is perfect sensibility of the measure of danger, and a mental willingness to endure it.

— Gen. William T. Sherman

Bravery never goes out of fashion.

— William M. Thackeray

Do your duty and leave the rest to providence.

— Andrew "Stonewall" Jackson

ea, though I walk
through the valley of
the shadow of death I
shall fear no evil.
Thou art with me, thy rod and
thy staff, they comfort me.

— *Psalm 23*